dabblelab

PAPER AIRPLANES
with a SIDE of SCIENCE

SPACE BOMBER!

EXPERT-LEVEL
Paper Airplanes

by Marie Buckingham

4D An Augmented Reading
Paper-Folding Experience

CAPSTONE PRESS
a capstone imprint

TABLE OF

CONTENTS

Download the Capstone 4D app!

Step 1 Ask an adult to search in the Apple App Store or Google Play for "Capstone 4D."

Step 2 Click Install (Android) or Get, then Install (Apple).

Step 3 Open the app.

Step 4 Scan any of the following spreads with this icon. - - - ▶ ★

When you scan a spread, you'll find fun extra stuff to go with this book! You can also find these things on the web at *www.capstone4D.com* using the password: planes.bomber

COMMAND THE SKIES

Congratulations on making the rank of captain! You have hours of flight experience under your belt. Now it's time to take command. Refresh your knowledge by checking the lightbulb boxes tucked alongside the paper airplane instructions for bite-size explanations of flight-science concepts related to your models. Check the photo boxes for tips on how to best launch your finished planes. There are four main forces that airplanes need to fly successfully: lift, weight, thrust, and drag. But the seven paper airplanes in this book need one more thing: YOU!

MATERIALS

Every paper airplane builder needs a well-stocked
toolbox. The models in this book use the materials
listed below. Take a minute before you begin folding
to gather what you need:

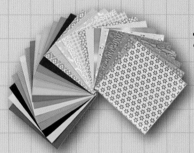

Paper

Any paper you can fold will work.
Notebook paper is always popular. But
paper with cool colors and designs gives
your planes style.

Scissors

Keep a scissors handy. Some models need
a snip here or there to fly well.

TECHNIQUES AND TERMS

Folding paper airplanes isn't difficult when you understand common folding techniques and terms. Review this list before folding the models in this book. Remember to refer back to this list if you get stuck on a tricky step.

Valley Folds

Valley folds are represented by a dashed line. The paper is creased along the line. The top surface of the paper is folded against itself like a book.

Mountain Folds

Mountain folds are represented by a pink or white dashed and dotted line. The paper is creased along the line and folded behind.

Reverse Folds

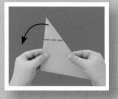  

Reverse folds are made by opening a pocket slightly and folding the model inside itself along existing creases.

Mark Folds

Mark folds are light folds used to make reference creases for a later step. Ideally, a mark fold will not be seen in the finished model.

Rabbit Ear Folds

Rabbit ear folds are formed by bringing two edges of a point together using existing creases. The new point is folded to one side.

Squash Folds

Squash folds are formed by lifting one edge of a pocket and reforming it so the spine gets flattened. The existing creases become new edges.

FOLDING SYMBOLS

Fold the paper in the direction of the arrow.

Fold the paper behind.

Fold the paper and then unfold it.

Turn the paper over or rotate it to a new position.

• • • • • • • • • • • • •

A fold or edge hidden under another layer of paper; also used to mark where to cut with a scissors

FIGHTER JET

Traditional Model

Want a fighter jet that is always ready for its next military mission? This stylish plane swoops through the air. It's a great flier that looks super cool.

Materials

* 6.5- by 11-inch (16.5- by 28-centimeter) paper

START HERE

1 Valley fold edge to edge and unfold.

2 Valley fold in half.

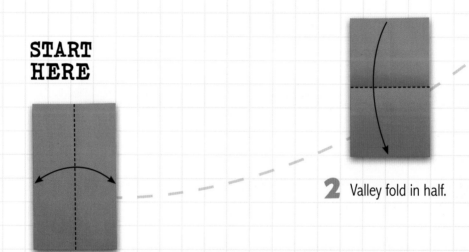

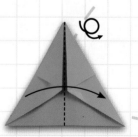

7 Valley fold the model in half and rotate.

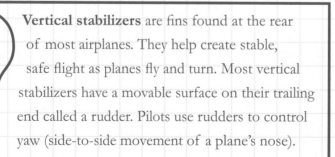

Vertical stabilizers are fins found at the rear of most airplanes. They help create stable, safe flight as planes fly and turn. Most vertical stabilizers have a movable surface on their trailing end called a rudder. Pilots use rudders to control yaw (side-to-side movement of a plane's nose).

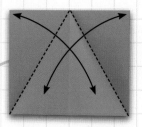

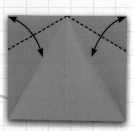

4 Valley fold the corners to the creases made in step 3 and unfold.

3 Valley fold the corners and unfold. Note how creases run from the center to the bottom corners.

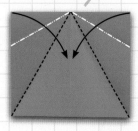

5 Squash fold using the creases made in steps 3 and 4.

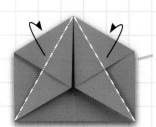

6 Mountain fold on the existing creases.

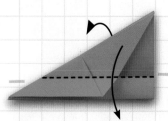

8 Valley fold the top layer. Repeat behind.

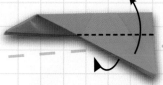

9 Valley fold the top flap of the wing. Repeat behind.

Continue ▶

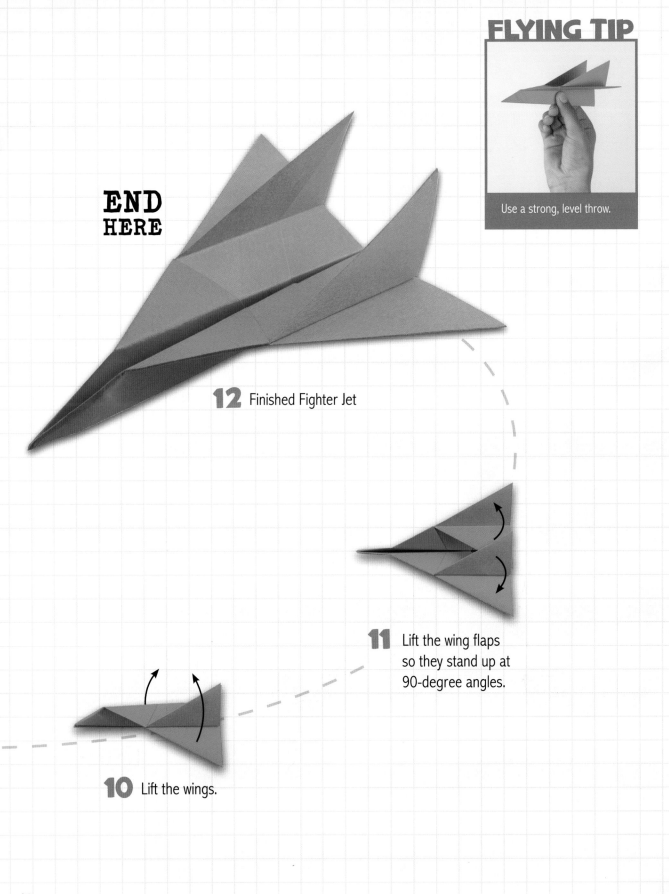

Use a strong, level throw.

END HERE

12 Finished Fighter Jet

11 Lift the wing flaps so they stand up at 90-degree angles.

10 Lift the wings.

⭐ WARTHOG

Designed by Christopher L. Harbo

The Warthog is a beast. It may not be pretty, but this little glider soars long distances through the air. Don't worry about hitting the wall. The Warthog's snub nose can take a beating.

Materials

* 8.5- by 11-inch (22- by 28-cm) paper

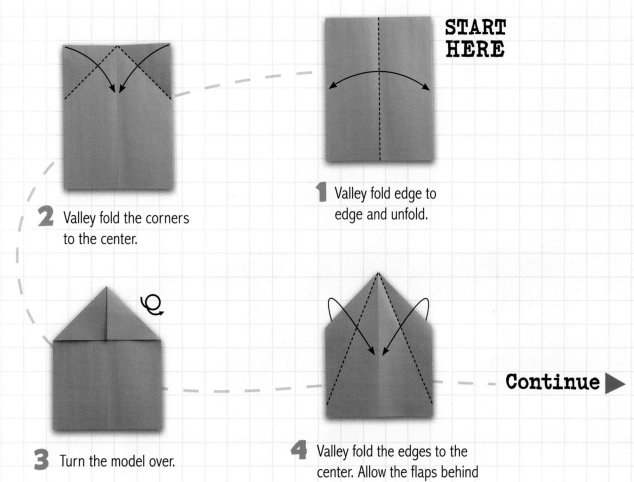

START HERE

1 Valley fold edge to edge and unfold.

2 Valley fold the corners to the center.

3 Turn the model over.

4 Valley fold the edges to the center. Allow the flaps behind to release to the top.

Continue ▶

11

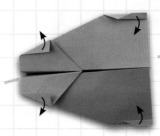

12 Lift the top layer of the wing flaps and the nose flaps so they stand up at 90-degree angles.

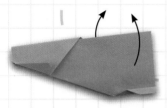

11 Lift the wings.

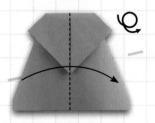

10 Valley fold the wing flap. Repeat behind.

FLYING TIP

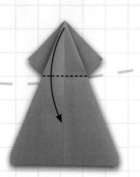

Use a strong, level throw.

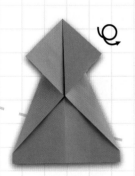

5 Turn the model over.

6 Valley fold the point.

7 Valley fold the model in half and rotate.

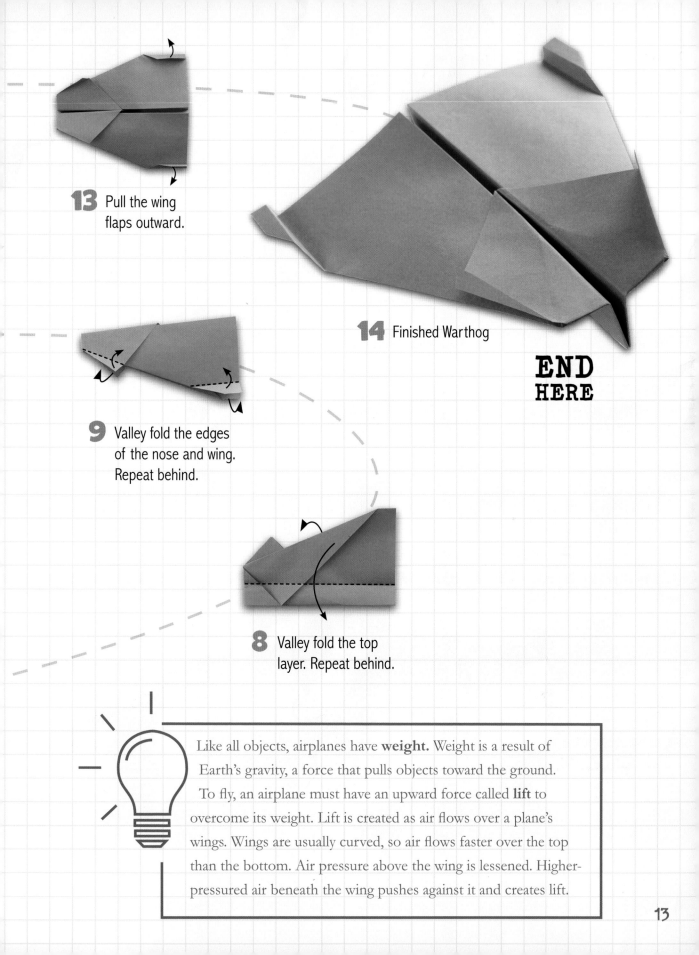

13 Pull the wing flaps outward.

14 Finished Warthog

END HERE

9 Valley fold the edges of the nose and wing. Repeat behind.

8 Valley fold the top layer. Repeat behind.

Like all objects, airplanes have **weight.** Weight is a result of Earth's gravity, a force that pulls objects toward the ground. To fly, an airplane must have an upward force called **lift** to overcome its weight. Lift is created as air flows over a plane's wings. Wings are usually curved, so air flows faster over the top than the bottom. Air pressure above the wing is lessened. Higher-pressured air beneath the wing pushes against it and creates lift.

GLIDING GRACE

Designed by Christopher L. Harbo

Flying the Gliding Grace takes a soft touch. Throw it too hard and it goes into a steep dive. But a smooth, medium throw sends this model soaring. It's the perfect plane to practice your launching skills.

Materials

* 8.5- by 11-inch (22- by 28-cm) paper

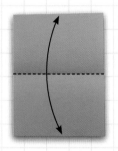

START HERE

1 Valley fold in half and unfold.

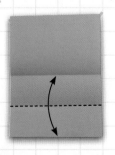

2 Valley fold to the center and unfold.

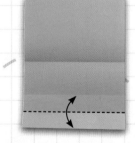

3 Valley fold to the crease made in step 2 and unfold.

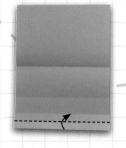

4 Valley fold to the crease made in step 3.

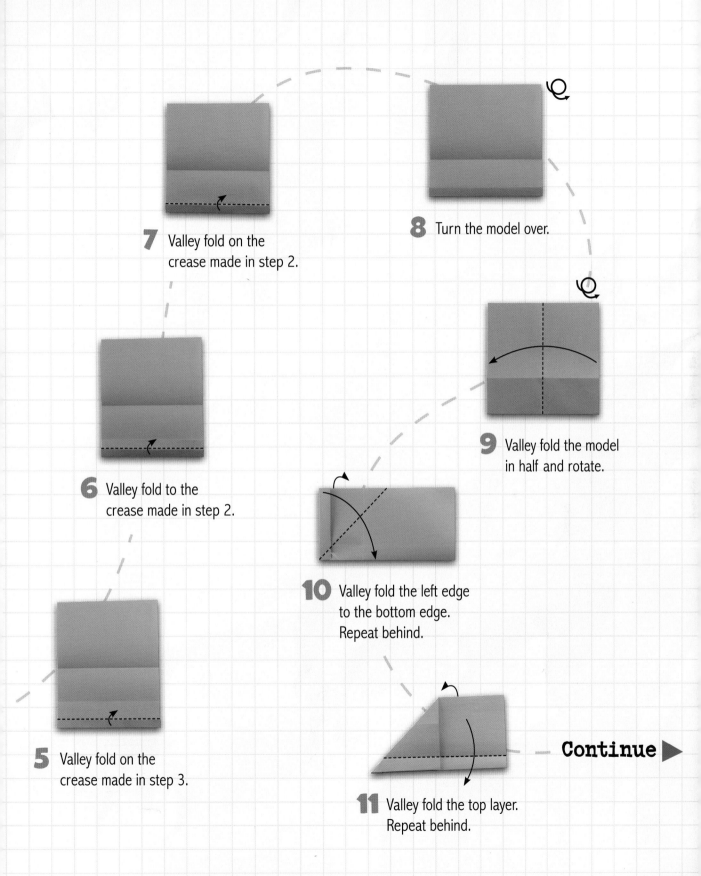

7 Valley fold on the crease made in step 2.

8 Turn the model over.

9 Valley fold the model in half and rotate.

6 Valley fold to the crease made in step 2.

10 Valley fold the left edge to the bottom edge. Repeat behind.

5 Valley fold on the crease made in step 3.

11 Valley fold the top layer. Repeat behind.

Continue ▶

15

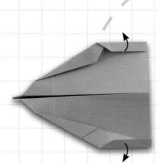

16 Lift the wing flaps so they stand up at 90-degree angles.

17 Finished Gliding Grace

END HERE

FLYING TIP

Use a soft throw with a smooth, level release.

15 Lift the wings.

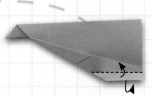

14 Valley fold the edge of the wing. Repeat behind.

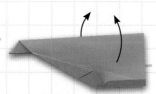

13 Valley fold to the crease. Repeat behind.

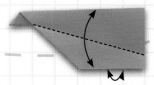

12 Valley fold the wing even with the top edge and unfold. Repeat behind.

Increasing the speed of an airplane also increases its **drag**. As a plane moves faster, air molecules have a more difficult time moving out of the plane's way. Just like snow piles up in front of a snowplow, air molecules pile up near a wing's front edge at fast speeds and create drag.

FLYING ACCORDION

Traditional Model

Can a paper plane with so many peaks and valleys really fly? Fold the Flying Accordion and find out. This unique glider will have your friends begging you to make them one.

Materials

* 8.5- by 11-inch (22- by 28-cm) paper

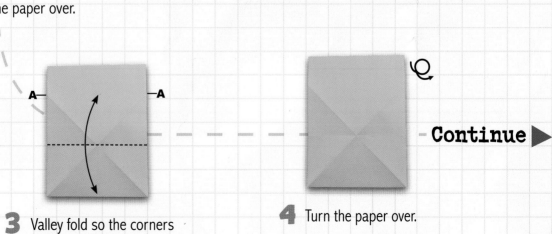

START HERE

1 Valley fold edge to edge and unfold.

2 Turn the paper over.

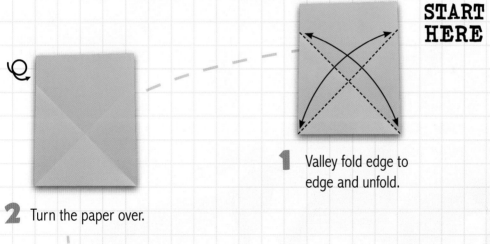

3 Valley fold so the corners meet at point A and unfold.

4 Turn the paper over.

Continue ▶

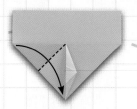

10 Repeat steps 6 through 9 on the left side.

11 Mountain fold the point.

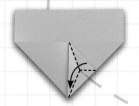

9 Rabbit ear fold on the creases formed in steps 7 and 8.

FLYING TIP

Pinch the plane on the triangle beneath its wings. Give it a medium, level throw.

8 Valley fold to the center and unfold.

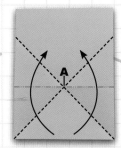

5 Push at point A. Collapse the paper on the existing creases to form a triangle.

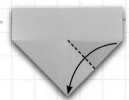

6 Valley fold the top layer to the point.

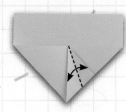

7 Valley fold to the center and unfold.

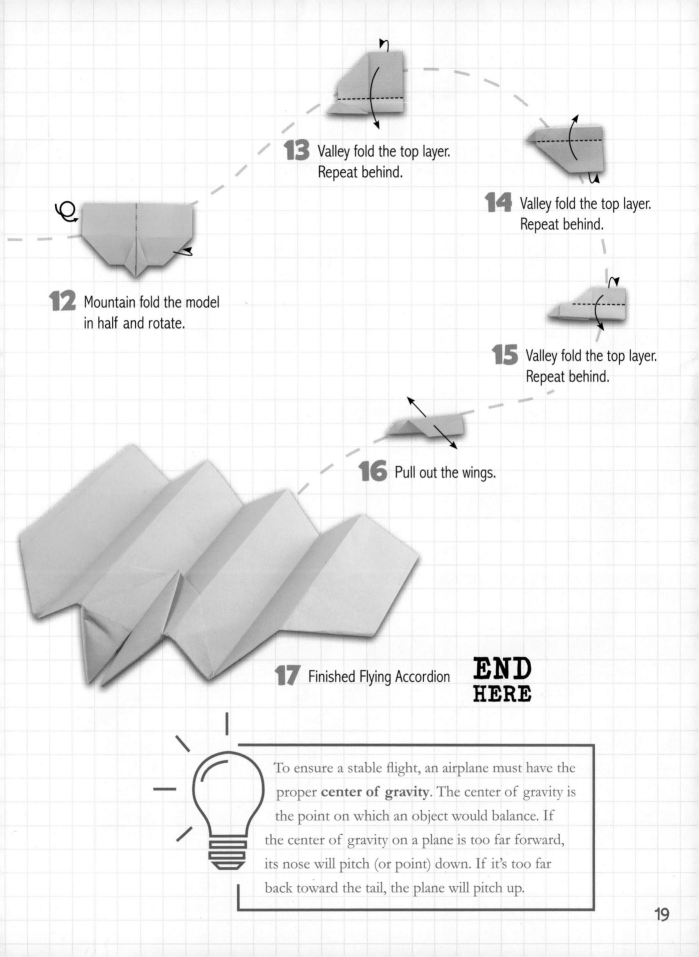

13 Valley fold the top layer. Repeat behind.

14 Valley fold the top layer. Repeat behind.

12 Mountain fold the model in half and rotate.

15 Valley fold the top layer. Repeat behind.

16 Pull out the wings.

17 Finished Flying Accordion

END HERE

To ensure a stable flight, an airplane must have the proper **center of gravity**. The center of gravity is the point on which an object would balance. If the center of gravity on a plane is too far forward, its nose will pitch (or point) down. If it's too far back toward the tail, the plane will pitch up.

⭐ SPACE BOMBER

Traditional Model

The Space Bomber looks like it flew in from another world. Don't let this plane's boxy shape fool you. Its flight paths are amazingly straight and long.

Materials

* 8.5- by 11-inch (22- by 28-cm) paper

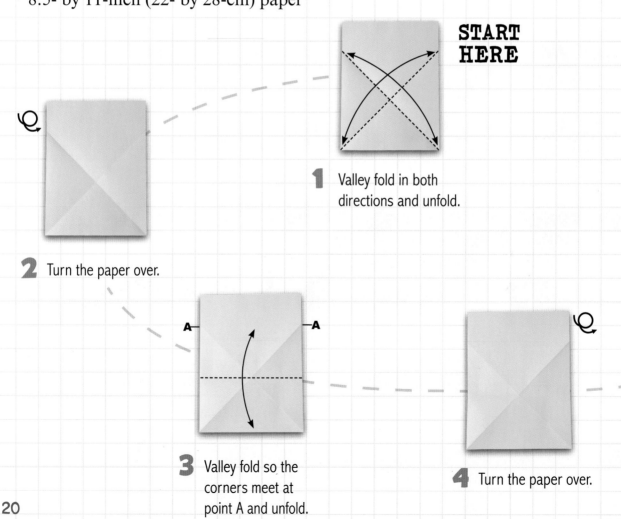

START HERE

1 Valley fold in both directions and unfold.

2 Turn the paper over.

3 Valley fold so the corners meet at point A and unfold.

4 Turn the paper over.

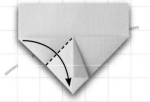

8 Repeat steps 6 and 7 on the left side.

9 Valley fold the point.

FLYING TIP

Pinch the plane on the triangle beneath the wings. Give it a medium, level throw.

7 Valley fold to the center.

10 Unfold the two flaps beneath the point.

6 Valley fold the top layer to the point.

11 Tuck the flaps into the pockets of the point.

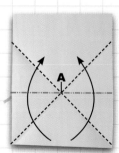

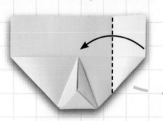

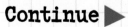

5 Push at point A. Collapse the paper on the existing creases to form a triangle.

12 Valley fold to the center.

Continue ▶

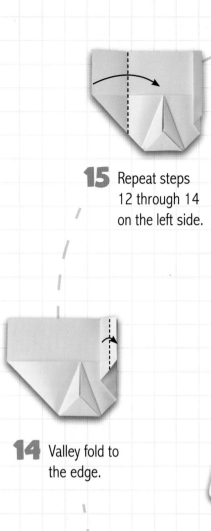

15 Repeat steps 12 through 14 on the left side.

16 Pull the edges of the wings out to create U-shaped channels. Turn the model over.

14 Valley fold to the edge.

17 Finished Space Bomber

END HERE

13 Valley fold to the edge.

As airplanes soar through Earth's atmosphere, four forces affect them: weight, lift, drag, and thrust. **Space flight** is quite different. Because there is no air to move over wings, there is also no lift or drag. Only two forces act upon spacecraft in flight: weight and thrust.

⭐ SPARROWHAWK

Traditional Model

Do you want the Sparrowhawk to sail like a glider or loop around like a stunt plane? Changing the power and angle of your throw will determine how this plane flies. Either way, the Sparrowhawk doesn't disappoint.

Materials

* 8.5- by 11-inch (22- by 28-cm) paper

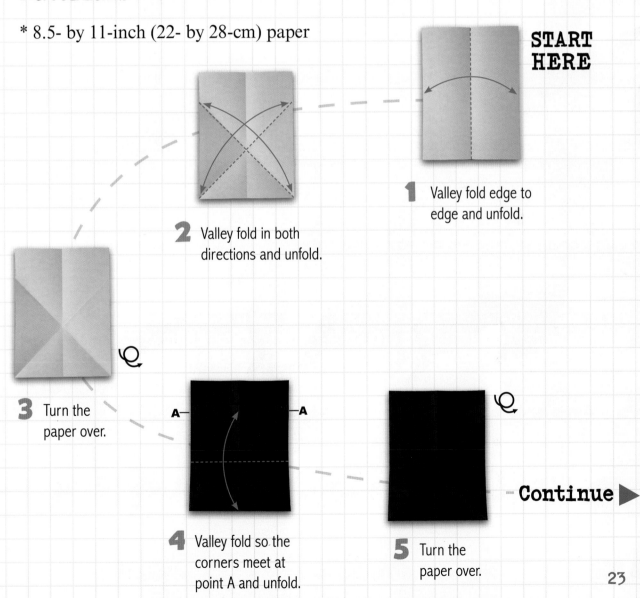

START HERE

1 Valley fold edge to edge and unfold.

2 Valley fold in both directions and unfold.

3 Turn the paper over.

4 Valley fold so the corners meet at point A and unfold.

5 Turn the paper over.

Continue ▶

23

9 Valley fold to the center and unfold.

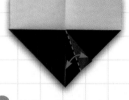

8 Valley fold to the center and unfold.

10 Rabbit ear fold on the creases formed in steps 8 and 9.

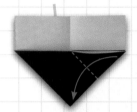

7 Valley fold the top layer to the point.

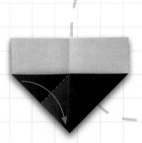

11 Repeat steps 7 through 10 on the left side.

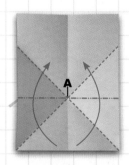

A

6 Push at point A. Collapse the paper on the existing creases to form a triangle.

All airplanes need a force called **thrust** to fly. Gas- and electric-powered engines produce thrust for full-size planes. The push of a hand or a rubber-band launcher gives paper airplanes the thrust they need. Hang gliders get thrust from their pilots running and often jumping from a hill or cliff.

18 Finished Sparrowhawk

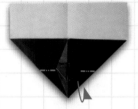

12 Mountain fold
the point.

13 Valley fold the
model in half
and rotate.

FLYING TIP

For smooth flights, give the plane
a medium, level throw. For stunt
flights, give it a hard throw with
a steep upward angle.

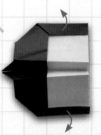

17 Lift the wing flaps
so they stand up at
90-degree angles.

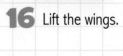

16 Lift the wings.

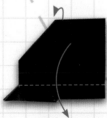

14 Valley fold
the top layer.
Repeat behind.

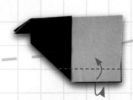

15 Valley fold
the top layer.
Repeat behind.

SCREECH OWL

Traditional Model

With its wide wings and narrow tail, the Screech Owl glides like a silent hunter. Hold it as high as you can to get the longest flight.

Materials

* 7- by 10.5-inch (18- by 27-cm) paper
* scissors

START HERE ✂

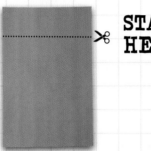

1 Cut a 2-inch (5-cm) strip off the end of the paper.

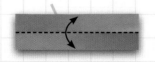

2 Valley fold the strip edge to edge and unfold.

3 Valley fold the corners of the strip to the center. Set aside.

4 Valley fold the large paper in both directions and unfold.

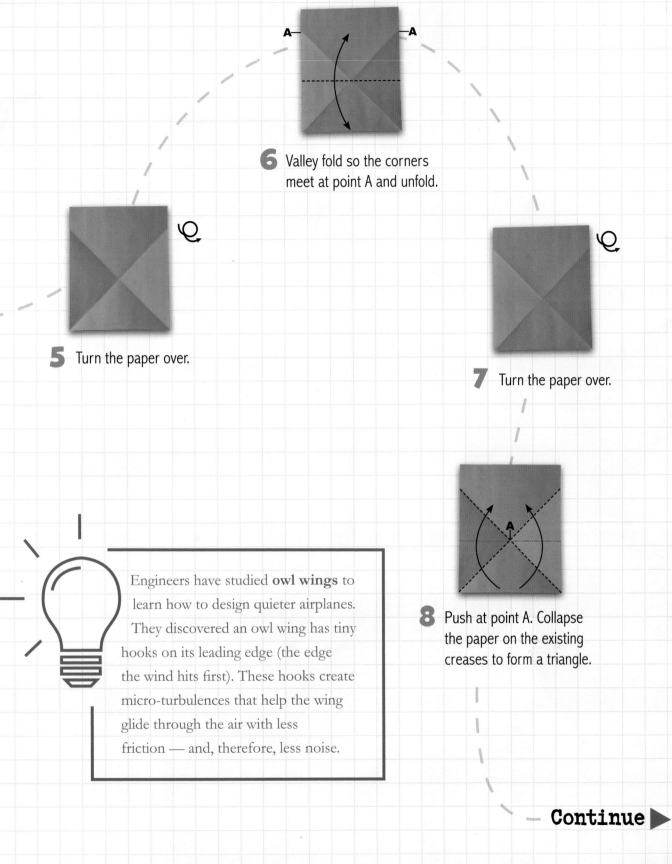

6 Valley fold so the corners meet at point A and unfold.

5 Turn the paper over.

7 Turn the paper over.

8 Push at point A. Collapse the paper on the existing creases to form a triangle.

Engineers have studied **owl wings** to learn how to design quieter airplanes. They discovered an owl wing has tiny hooks on its leading edge (the edge the wind hits first). These hooks create micro-turbulences that help the wing glide through the air with less friction — and, therefore, less noise.

Continue ▶

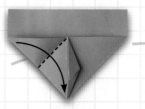

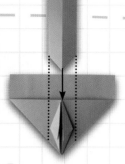

13 Repeat steps 9 through 12 on the left side.

14 Insert the strip between the layers so it fits in the point.

12 Rabbit ear fold on the creases formed in steps 10 and 11.

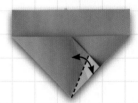

11 Valley fold to the center and unfold.

10 Valley fold to the center and unfold.

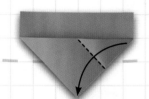

9 Valley fold the top layer to the point.

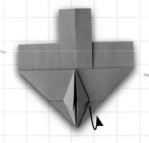

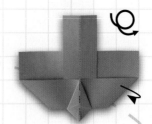

15 Mountain fold the point.

16 Mountain fold the model in half and rotate.

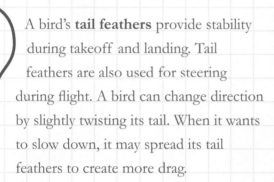

A bird's **tail feathers** provide stability during takeoff and landing. Tail feathers are also used for steering during flight. A bird can change direction by slightly twisting its tail. When it wants to slow down, it may spread its tail feathers to create more drag.

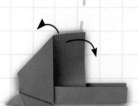

17 Lower the wings.

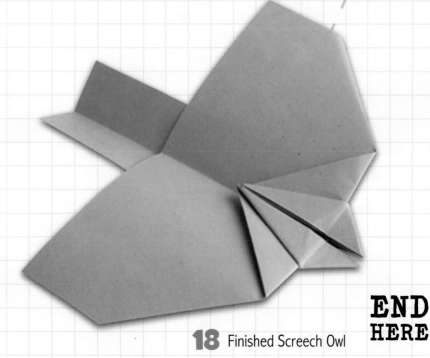

18 Finished Screech Owl

END HERE

⭐ INSIDE THE HANGAR:
STEALTH BOMBER

The B-2 Spirit stealth bomber is a flying-wing airplane. Like its name suggests, it looks like a big wing, without a definite body (fuselage) or tail. It measures 172 feet (52 meters) from wingtip to wingtip — about as long as an Olympic-sized swimming pool.

This powerful craft gets its thrust from four turbofan engines tucked inside its wings. It's designed to fly more than 6,000 nautical miles (6,905 miles; 11,112 kilometers) without refueling. (Note: Nautical miles are the standard measurement for air and sea travel. They're slightly longer than land miles.)

Perhaps the coolest part of the B-2 stealth bomber is its ability to hide. It's the perfect spy plane! Two design features work together to make the bomber difficult to see on radar. First, a radar-absorbent coating covers the exterior of the plane. The coating "eats" the radar signals so they can't report back. Second, the plane's shape is designed with a technique called continuous curvature. Radar signals bounce off the curved surface, into all sorts of directions.

Flying-wing aircraft, such as the B-2 Spirit stealth bomber, house all of their crew, fuel, and equipment inside one giant wing structure.

READ MORE

Collins, John M. *The New World Champion Paper Airplane Book: Featuring the Guinness World Record-Breaking Design, with Tear-Out Planes to Fold and Fly.* New York: Ten Speed Press, 2013.

LaFosse, Michael G. *Michael LaFosse's Origami Airplanes.* North Clarendon, Vt.: Tuttle Publishing, 2016.

Lee, Kyong Hwa. *Amazing Paper Airplanes: The Craft and Science of Flight.* Albuquerque, N.Mex.: University of New Mexico Press, 2016.

INTERNET SITES

Use FactHound to find Internet sites related to this book.

Visit *www.facthound.com*

Just type in 9781543507942 and go.

Special thanks to our adviser, Polly Kadolph, Associate Professor,
University of Dubuque (Iowa) Aviation Department, for her expertise.

Dabble Lab Books are published by Capstone Press,
1710 Roe Crest Drive, North Mankato, Minnesota 56003
www.mycapstone.com

Library of Congress Cataloging-in-Publication data is available on the Library of Congress website.
ISBN: 978-1-5435-0794-2 (library binding)
ISBN: 978-1-5435-0798-0 (eBook PDF)

Summary: Challenge yourself to fly faster and higher with these wild, expert-level paper airplane projects.
Step-by-step, 4D-supported instructions show you how to build the Space Bomber, the Sparrowhawk,
and more, while fact-filled sidebars and a special "Inside the Hangar" feature dive into the basic science
and engineering concepts related to flight.

Editorial Credits
Jill Kalz, editor; Heidi Thompson, designer; Eric Gohl, media researcher; Laura Manthe, production specialist

Photo Credits
Capstone Studio: Karon Dubke, all steps
Shutterstock: design elements, AMMHPhotography, 30

Printed in the United States of America.
010761S18